RUTH the SLEUTH
and the Messy Room

Written by Carol Gordon Ekster
Illustrated by Kimberly Soderberg

To all my critique buddies who helped me with this story.
I couldn't have done it without you.

To my mom, Ruth, who CAN find anything and everything she puts her mind to. And to my other mother, Sylvia.

Ruth the Sleuth and the Messy Room

Softcover (paper) ISBN: 978-1-946124-34-0
Hardcover (cloth) ISBN: 978-1-946124-33-3
Second Edition

Text Copyright © 2018 Carol Gordon Ekster

Published by
Mazo Publishers ~ P.O. Box 10474
Jacksonville, Florida 32247 USA
Tel: 1-815-301-3559

Website: www.mazopublishers.com
Email: mazopublishers@gmail.com

Library of Congress Cataloging-in-Publication Data

Ekster, Carol Gordon.
Ruth the Sleuth and the Messy Room/ written by Carol Ekster.

Summary: Ruth the Sleuth and the Messy Room is a children's picture book about a messy little girl who has misplaced her mother's potholder. She must find it in 10 minutes in order to have cookies and play with her friend, Zack. Includes a parent guide to raising organized children, and a checklist game to help kids learn to clean their rooms.

[1. Children's - Fiction. 2. General - Fiction. 3. Organization - Fiction.]

All Rights Reserved.
No part of this publication may be translated, reproduced, stored in a retrieval system, or transmitted in any form or by any means, electronic, mechanical, photocopying, recording or otherwise, without prior permission in writing from the publisher.

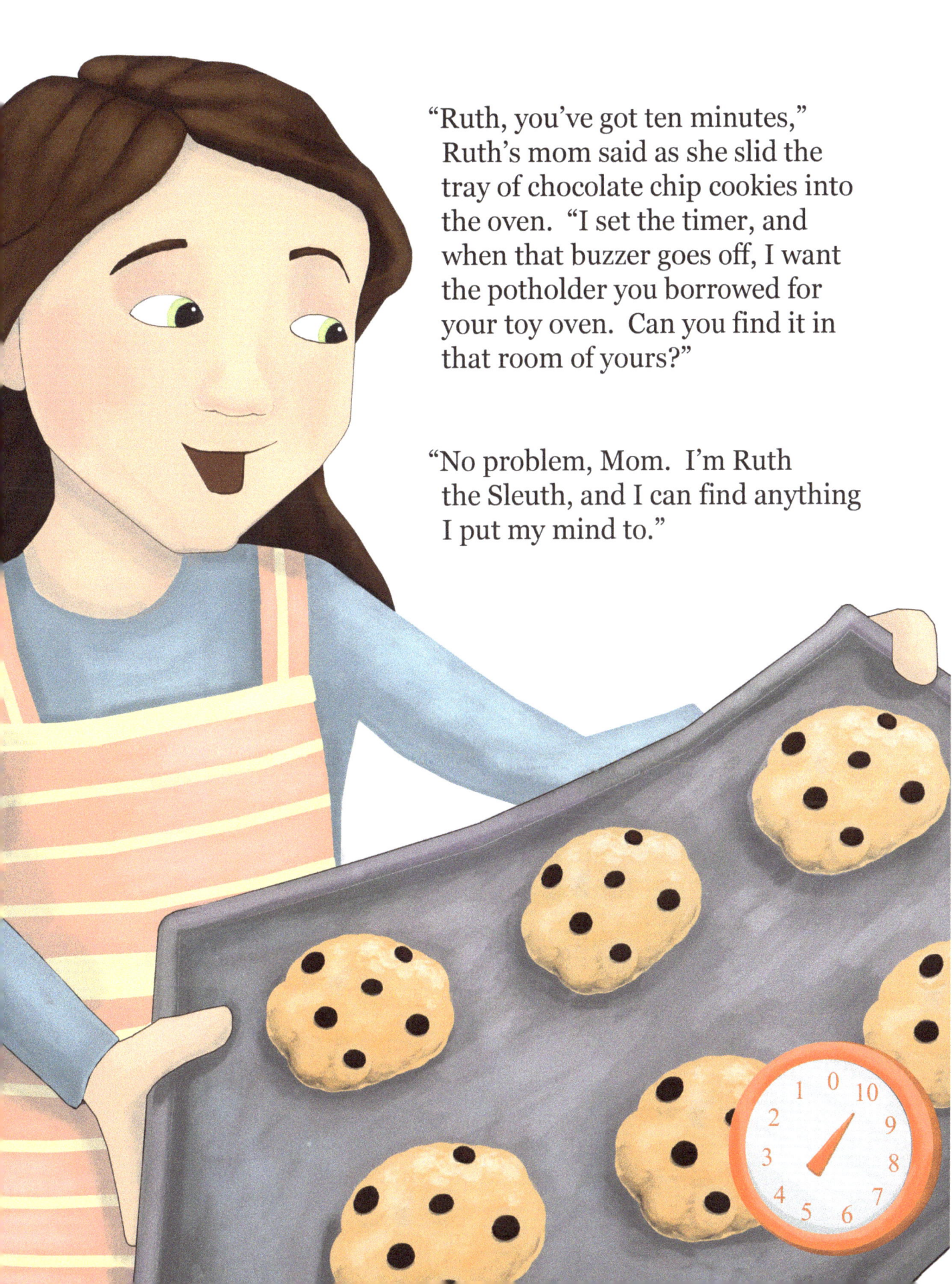

"Ruth, you've got ten minutes," Ruth's mom said as she slid the tray of chocolate chip cookies into the oven. "I set the timer, and when that buzzer goes off, I want the potholder you borrowed for your toy oven. Can you find it in that room of yours?"

"No problem, Mom. I'm Ruth the Sleuth, and I can find anything I put my mind to."

First, Ruth opened her toy oven. No potholder, but a shoelace from her old sneakers slipped out. She tied it around her head.

Next, Ruth slid under her bed, parting the sea of clothes and toys. She scanned the mess but did not spot the potholder. She slithered out, like a salamander sliding out from under a rock.

Ruth flipped over and stretched out her leg to reach the wastebasket. She tapped it with her toe, uncovering the blue crayon that had rolled away last week.

No potholder there. But the crayon begged to be used.

After a few scribbles, she dropped her picture on the floor.

She hopped over to the chair. It wouldn't rock. An eraser she had misplaced last week sat wedged underneath the rocker-rails. She scooped it up, shot it across the room, and made a basket!

At her desk, Ruth nudged a pile of papers. Her favorite book peeked out from under the heap. She flipped through a few pages, then tossed it over her shoulder.

That's when she noticed a yellow envelope at the edge of her desk with an old birthday card inside. When she opened the card, a neatly folded ten-dollar bill parachuted to the floor.

"Money, money, money!" Ruth sang as she danced around the piles.

When her celebration was finished, Ruth tunneled through the hill of shoes at the bottom of her closet. The potholder wasn't there, but she spied her very favorite sneakers from last year in the corner.

She squinched her eyes shut and made a wish. Then she blew off the thick layer of dust. Little dust fairies scattered around her head.

She shoved her toes into the too-tight sneakers and shuffled off to track down the potholder.

"Where could it be?" she wondered. "I'm Ruth the Sleuth, and I can find anything I put my mind to. Wasn't I the one who always found Mr. Zucker's reading glasses? Didn't I find Madison's lunch card, when no one else could? Who needs organized drawers and closets?

NOT ME!"

"Ruth," Mom called, "you have a visitor." It was Ruth's new neighbor. "Hey, Zack."

"Hey, Ruth. Wanna come out and play?"

"Okay," Ruth answered. Mom shook her head. "Sorry, Zack, Ruth is working on something for me."

Ruth asked, "Mom, can Zack come in and help me?"

"Sure. But it's such a nice day, maybe Zack would rather be outside."

"I'll help," Zack offered.

He stepped into her bedroom and giggled. "Wow! It looks like a giant vacuum threw up in here."

"I love my room!" Ruth frowned.

Zack jumped into one of the piles, dove into another, and then rolled around the stuff covering the floor.

He brushed himself off, and announced, "Gotta go."

Ruth's shoulders slumped. "Maybe I'll see you in a few minutes."

Ruth heard the door close.
Suddenly, she wanted fresh air more than a hungry dog wanted treats.

She decided to write a note on her reminder board, to make better piles to find things more easily.
But the marker for her dry-erase board wasn't hanging on its hook.

"Ruth! Two minutes left," Mom warned.

"I'm on the case," Ruth shouted.

Ruth crouched down under the desk and felt around the mounds of toys to see if it had dropped there.

Ow!

No marker, but she felt something sharp poke her tummy. A little scrape wouldn't stop Ruth!

She pulled at the top desk drawer, but it was too stuffed with papers to open. She grabbed it with both hands and yanked as hard as she could.

Ouch!
Her finger throbbed with a splinter.

She stretched over the desk to look behind it. There, sticking out from under her bicycle helmet, was Mom's potholder.

"Wahoo!!" Ruth cheered. "I got it!"

The buzzer blasted.

BEEP!
BEEP!
BEEP!

Ruth zoomed into the kitchen, curtsied, and handed over the potholder, just as heat shot out of the opened oven door.

"I'm Ruth the Sleuth, and I can find anything I put my mind to. And now I'm off to find my friend."

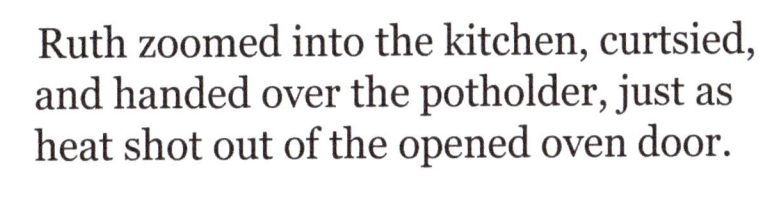

Ruth's Favorite Chocolate Chip Cookies:

1 cup brown sugar
1 cup unsweetened apple sauce
1 large egg white
2 tbls canola oil
1 tbls vanilla
1 cup chocolate chips
2 cups rolled oats
1 1/2 cups whole wheat flour
1 tsp baking soda
1/2 tsp salt

Preheat oven to 350 degrees. Wisk sugar, applesauce, eggwhite, oil, and vanilla in a large bowl until smooth.

Then mix all dry ingredients into wet mixture. Bake for 10 minutes, or until edges are golden-brown.

Allow cookies to cool for 10 minutes before trying to remove them from the pan.

Enjoy!

A Parent's Guide to Growing Organized Kids

Are you having trouble motivating your children into keeping their rooms clean? Perhaps the following timed-checklist game will help. The game encourages children to stay organized and tidy by
1. Setting clear, general goals to help them with the hardest part... deciding where to begin.
2. Hand-holding children through each step of the cleaning process, allowing for an instant result (an actual time to write down) at the end of each step.
3. Strategically placing the quicker/easier tasks (throwing away trash pile, bringing laundry to correct area, carrying items to correct rooms) in the middle of the harder processes to keep children motivated and encouraged.
4. Giving kids an opportunity to stay motivated by pre-scheduling a chance to play the game again, and to beat her previous time!

Please note that if you let your child take the lead in this process, and if you reward each improvement, you are more likely to develop the lifelong skills of organization, self-motivation, and time-management. Otherwise, your results will be only short-lived. Suggestions for letting your child take the lead include:
1. Letting her decide where things should go in a clean room. Although you can certainly make suggestions, and troubleshoot major strategy-flaws (such as keeping all clean laundry under her bed), you should try to keep an opened mind about the placement of items...even if it makes you cringe each time you walk in to see her earrings duct-taped to her Hanna Montana poster. The more she feels like she owns an idea, the more likely she is to implement (or improve) it.
2. Letting your child decide how often she wants to schedule room cleaning. You may be surprised how much more likely a child is to learn from her own experiences (especially when she can see the results clearly herself on this checklist) than from advice based on a parent's life-experiences.

In other words, instead of saying, "That is a bad idea, because you will have to spend all day cleaning if you only do it once per month." Try saying, "Good idea! Let's mark the calendar for a cleaning in a month. Should we also schedule a sooner time to see which way is faster? How soon?"

When in doubt, change your wording into the form of a question.

Suggestions for rewards may include:
1. A sticker on a chart
2. A certain number of minutes (you could match the minutes of time-shaved-off of previous cleaning time) of any of the following:

    Mommy/Daddy-and-me time (no siblings allowed)
    TV/Video game extras
    Cooking/Baking/Craft/Creativity/Reading time (whatever your child likes best)

3. A friend over to play in the freshly-cleaned room
4. Ruth the Sleuth's chocolate chip cookies! See recipe on last page.

How to Use the Timing Game

Use the timed-sections to decide which portions of room-tidiness take up the most time/need the most work to become less of a nuisance. Please note: try to make this activity fun, and your child will rise to the occasion, eventually keeping her own room tidy without you asking.

Also, don't try to correct all of the problem-areas at once, as this will overwhelm your child. Simply focus on one area per week or month.

Ruth the Sleuth's Room Tidiness Questionnaire:

How long do you think it takes to clean up your room? (check one)
☐ 10 minutes?
☐ 30 minutes?
☐ A whole hour?
☐ Longer than one hour? YIKES!

I guess the answer depends on how messy your room is. Try this one:

Which would you like better? (check one)
☐ To clean up your room for only five minutes each day?
☐ To clean up your room for 15 minutes, but only three days each week?
☐ To clean up your room for a whole hour, but only once per week?

Did you notice that the more often you clean up your room, the less time it takes?

6 Steps to a Clean Room
Do you want to try an experiment to find out how long it really takes to clean your room? Ask a grown up to help you with timing. Then bring the checklist below to your room. Ask a parent to time each section, and then add up your times at the bottom.

Step 1: Make five piles:

Ready. Set. Go!

☐ Clean clothes   ☐ Dirty clothes   ☐ Things to put away   ☐ Things that don't belong in my room   ☐ Trash

How long did Step 1 take?   Step 1 Time: _____Minutes_____Seconds

Step 2: Throw the trash away.
Ready. Set. Go!
How long did Step 2 take?   Step 2 Time: _____Minutes_____Seconds

Step 3: Bring the dirty laundry to the laundry area of the house.
Ready. Set. Go!
How long did Step 3 take?   Step 3 Time:_____Minutes_____Seconds

Step 4:   Fold or hang clean clothes, and put them away.
Ready. Set. Go!
How long did Step 4 take?   Step 4 Time: _____Minutes_____Seconds

Step 5: Carry everything that doesn't belong in your room to the rooms they belong in, and give them back to their owners, or put them away yourself.
Ready. Set. Go!
How long did Step 5 take?   Step 5 Time: _____Minutes_____Seconds

Step 6: Put the things in your last pile where you would like them to go in your room.
Ready. Set. Go!
How long did Step 2 take?   Step 6 Time:_____Minutes_____Seconds

                    Total Cleaning Time:_____Minutes_____Seconds

Do you think you can do it faster next time? How soon will you try it?

Next Scheduled Game _____

Author Bio

Carol Gordon Ekster was a passionate teacher for the Derry New Hampshire school system. She read picture books aloud to her students every day, not realizing she was also preparing herself to become an author. Carol retired after teaching 4th grade for 35 years. She now enjoys, exercising, practicing yoga, writing, and promoting her books. She is grateful that her writing gives her a way to continue communicating with children. She lives in Andover, MA with her husband Mark.

Illustrator Bio

Kimberly Soderberg was born and raised in Northern Ohio. As a little girl, she always loved to be creative. From doodles on paper to hand made kites, she was always engaged in a project. Her love for art grew, and she found herself at the Columbus College of Art & Design, where she received her bachelor's degree. She lives in Cleveland with her husband, Josh, her son, Wyatt, and her two furry dogs, Ralphie and Gertie.

How the Art Was Made

Ruth the Sleuth and the Messy Room was created using a modern technique called digital painting. The pages were first sketched out with a pencil. After Kim was satisfied with her pencil-drawings, she scanned them into the computer, and then used a special painting program to add color and texture right onto the computer screen!

www.ingramcontent.com/pod-product-compliance
Lightning Source LLC
Chambersburg PA
CBHW041433040426
42451CB00021B/3494